Acclaim for

YOUR NEXT BIG CAREER MOVE

"Let's be real: Job searching is the absolute worst. Instead of dwelling on the process, *Your Next Big Career Move* provides intuitive and practical prompts to move you forward with confidence. A welcome antidote to uncertainty, this journal offers a cathartic place to work through your feelings about your future, discover what you really want from your next job, and become brave enough to go after it."
—KARA CUTRUZZULA, author of *Do It For Yourself, Do It Today,* and *Do It (or Don't)*

"It's like a career coach at your fingertips providing valuable structure, perspectives, and prompts to help guide you through your journey."
—NICOLA RIES TAGGART, author of *Calm the Chaos Journal* and *Write and Release Journal*

"I wish I had this book years ago between jobs. It will help you not only with the search and interview stages but also the hardest part: the waiting. In *Your Next Big Career Move*, you'll find fresh ideas to increase your value, build your skill set, and gain control of your next step. There's lots to do before you're hired, so get moving!"
—D.A. SARAC, author of the self-care series *Big F*cking Dreams, Love This F*cking Journey,* and *I am F*cking Radiant*

"Cara Bedick's ninety-nine practical and inspiring prompts and friendly tone make it easy for current and aspiring job seekers to make strategic career decisions with confidence. Make sure your next big career move includes this welcome guide."
—KAREN WICKRE, author of *Taking the Work Out of Networking*

"*Your Next Big Career Move* is a thoughtful companion for one of life's most challenging transitions. Cara Bedick gently guides readers through the often-overwhelming experience of searching for a new job, offering structure, reflection, and, above all, hope. Combining wise and practical advice, the book can help readers transform uncertainty into opportunity and anxiety into purposeful action."
—TAL BEN-SHAHAR, author of *Happier* and *Choose the Life You Want* and founder of the Happiness Studies Academy

"Every job seeker needs this journal. It's easy to get lost in endless soul-searching or jump into tactical job search activities without clarity on what we actually want. Bedick bridges that gap, offering prompts that balance introspection with action-taking and move you closer to your next opportunity with each reflection."
—MELODY WILDING, LMSW, author of *Managing Up* and *Trust Yourself*

"As job stress and uncertainty reach a fever pitch for so many, *Your Next Big Career Move* shines like a light in the darkness. With insight, warmth, and invaluable expertise, it offers concrete guidance for those seeking help in charting their professional path."
—ANDREA BONIOR, PhD, author of *Detox Your Thoughts* and professor of psychology at Georgetown University

YOUR NEXT BIG CAREER MOVE

A Guided Journal for Job Seekers

CARA BEDICK

THE EXPERIMENT
NEW YORK

Your Next Big Career Move: *A Guided Journal for Job Seekers*

The Experiment, LLC
220 East 23rd Street, Suite 600
New York, NY 10010-4658
theexperimentpublishing.com

Library of Congress Cataloging-in-Publication Data available upon request

ISBN 979-8-89303-100-3
Ebook ISBN 979-8-89303-101-0

Cover and text design by Beth Bugler
Author photograph courtesy of the author

Manufactured in the United States of America

First printing January 2026
10 9 8 7 6 5 4 3 2 1

The authorized representative in the EU for product safety and compliance is
Easy Access System Europe, Mustamäe tee 50, 10621 Tallinn, Estonia
easproject.com | gpsr.requests@easproject.com

This journal is for anyone wondering
"Now what?"
I promise that you will figure it out.

CONTENTS

Introduction 1
Ways to Use This Journal 5

1 **What You Want from Your Next Big Career Move** 9
1. Introspection 11
2. Goal Setting 21
3. Exploration 33
4. Dream Job 43

2 **What You Need to Make Your Next Big Career Move** 55
5. Resume Building 57
6. Connection 67
7. Interview Skills 77

3 **How You Stay Focused on Your Next Big Career Move** 87
8. Motivation 89
9. Confidence 97
10. Gratitude 107
11. Adaptability 117

Your Next Big Career Move Is Up to You 129
Notes 131
Acknowledgments 134
About the Author 136

INTRODUCTION

On average it takes three to six months to land a job.[1] The search itself can feel like full-time work—scanning listings, updating your resume, curating a cover letter, submitting an application, interviewing, and more—but there's also a ton of lag time. It's normal to want to feel like you're being more productive while you wait to hear back from HR, interviews, and for an offer. This journal is a collection of job-hunting tips and self-examining questions, and a useful source of structure. Whether you're reentering the job market after a layoff, career setback, or a prolonged leave, entering the job market for the first time, or simply exploring your options, *Your Next Big Career Move* will guide you on your way toward wherever you are headed.

This is meant to be is an immersive experience, guided by exercises that inspire introspection, discovery, and action. Each chapter features prompts that serve to build you up while strengthening the very skills (assessment, communication, sales, negotiation, self-confidence) that will help you secure your next role, one that is aligned with your strengths and values, and that you will be excited to begin.

The prompts will also provide structure for your search, an opportunity to work through your feelings, and improve your perspective. This is your job search journey, and this journal is here to empower you to take control over this temporary moment in your life. Because it *will* be temporary. Wouldn't it be nice to look back on this time and know that you used it to the fullest?

How This Journal Came to Be

I've worked in publishing, a highly competitive industry known for its thin margins and frequent reorgs, for more than twenty years. My resume may show one linear path from Editorial Assistant to Executive Editor (at time of publication), but there have been ups, downs, plenty of job changes, and side hustles that have all played a role in getting me to where I am. Now mid-career, I have held twelve titles across ten companies. Those numbers go up if you're counting the summer and part-time gigs of my youth—things like Concessions (Beer Slinger) and Veterinarian's Office Assistant.

I've navigated job searches as someone new to the market, as someone seeking a change, and as someone navigating a layoff (twice). The first time I was laid off, around the time of the Great Recession, I was in my twenties. I cried, signed the severance agreement immediately (I didn't know any better!), went back to my desk, answered emails, wrote a cringeworthy Facebook post, packed up my things, and went home.

The second time, I was in my forties, with a mortgage to pay and responsibility for my family's health insurance. I cried, took my time to review and negotiate the severance agreement, kept working until the very last day (commitment or denial?), and didn't sleep well for the next month-plus because I kept waking in the middle of the night thinking, "Now what?"

My circumstances and stages of life differed, but the feelings and the process of working through those feelings while figuring out what came next were very similar—and served as the impetus for this journal.

After my first layoff, I took long walks. I enrolled in a creative writing class at the Brooklyn Public Library. I helped a television personality write a book proposal. I was motivated and going through the motions of applying for jobs, but I was also filled with self-doubt and considered leaving the field where I had spent the past four and a half years putting in my dues. So I searched widely, applying to positions in fields I had never considered before. I might have become a recycling education coordinator, a high school guidance counselor, or a marketing associate. Sometimes a total career pivot is a fantastic choice. In my case, researching different fields opened my eyes to other options and reinforced my belief that publishing was the path for me.

Following my second layoff, I took even longer walks. I baked . . . a lot. I walked to 105th and Broadway to try some of the best pizza in NYC. With more years of experience under my belt, I had confidence in my skills, but doubts lingered. Would I find the right job, one I really wanted? Would my age/being mid-career limit my options? I had an amazing network and support system, but still I worried. And there's only so much applying for jobs, following up, and checking in with your network you can do each day.

I needed something more to do. I challenged myself to try new things. I researched resiliency and communication. I came up with all sorts of ways to fill the time and master the search. This self-exploration helped me work through how I was feeling, which I knew would serve me once I decided what I was actually going to do next. And as I got closer to making that next move, I realized the things I had learned during the process could be helpful to others.

Your Job Search Journey

I hope *Your Next Big Career Move* will become a much-loved resource that you feel relieved to have discovered and empowered by using. You might be working through the grief commonly experienced along with a layoff, feeling uncertain about what comes next, or enthusiastically searching for your next opportunity. Regardless, it will get you through this transitional time.[2] It's packed with hard-won advice and reflection questions that will lift you up, assist you in organizing the days, and motivate you to make the moves to snag your next job—one that you can't wait to start—in record time.

The prompts in Part 1 will kick off your thinking about where you are and what you want. Part 2 gets more specific about skills-building. In Part 3, you'll address underlying factors that have a major effect on your job search—bolstering your confidence and keeping you moving forward until you snag something that's a strong and fulfilling fit. In each chapter I've condensed relevant and recent research into prompts for you to use as a springboard, intended to have you feeling productive and motivated.

Many of the exercises will ask you to go outside your comfort zone. You'll notice that each chapter includes a prompt encouraging you to *reach out to someone*—this is so important! Job searching can be a lonely time. Putting yourself out there can feel stressful at first, but connecting with others will ultimately boost your spirits. You'll learn something from every encounter and find that others are extremely willing to help.

Using the advice I'm now sharing in this journal, each time I was laid off, I landed a new job *before my severance ran out*. Whether you're on a specific job search timeline or just weighing your possibilities, *Your Next Big Career Move* will help you get through this period of searching, interviewing, waiting for the offer, and your start date. I'll be with you along the way with tips, tools, and practices to make the most of this time.

WAYS TO USE THIS JOURNAL

→

How you use this journal is completely up to you. The only requirement is that you actually use it. Cracking the spine of a journal and putting pen to paper for the first time can be intimidating—you want to put the right words down on the page. But there's nothing exact about this process. Your answers might change, and that's a good thing. You're evolving! All you have to do is start writing.* You can always change your mind, you can always update an entry, and hey, you can always get another copy. Here are a few different ways to think about how to approach the prompts.

As part of your "workday"

Structure your time by focusing on one prompt per day. Turn to it in the morning and use the prompt as a mantra for the day ahead, concentrating on its meaning and how it can be applied. Open it up midday after you've checked your email, the job boards, and LinkedIn. Or, in the late afternoon, devote a chunk of time to tackling whatever research, introspection, or outreach the prompt requests of you.

As a weekly check-in

Pick a day of the week; Fridays can be the worst for job seekers because they kick off a weekend of no news. But they can still be productive. Set aside an hour or more each Friday to sink into a number of prompts. Concentrating on this deep work will provide clarity on what you're really looking for.

As a skill-building or self-discovery master class

Some chapters are more technical (Resume Building), others more open-ended (Dream Job). All will teach you something about yourself that will be useful during your job search. If there's something specific you want to work on, head straight to the most relevant chapter.

With a job search group, networking club, or an accountability partner

Choose three questions (one from each part of the journal) to explore together. Share your answers and actively listen to each other. Focus on keeping your feedback supportive. If working with a larger group, breaking out into smaller groups of four or five will help to spark good conversation about where you're headed.

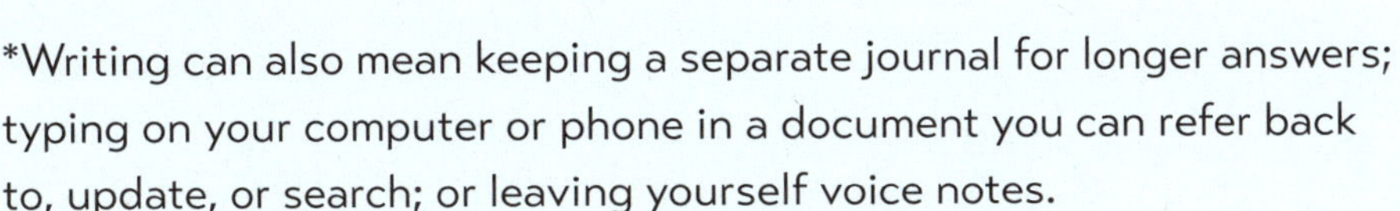

*Writing can also mean keeping a separate journal for longer answers; typing on your computer or phone in a document you can refer back to, update, or search; or leaving yourself voice notes.

1

WHAT YOU WANT FROM YOUR NEXT BIG CAREER MOVE

1

INTROSPECTION

Ask all the questions.

"You may ask yourself, *Well, how did I get here?"* The Talking Heads anthem could be a soundtrack to the early days of a job search. Your goal is to start digging up thoughts and ideas to help you make an informed decision about what comes next. Welcome to the research-gathering stage.

What's your work story? Describing your current work situation or simply answering the question "how's work?" doesn't need to be difficult. Remember that this is your story to tell. Take some time to write about what led you here, what details you want to share about your journey, and what you're looking for from your career in the future.

What do you value? It can be easy to get consumed with finding a job, any job, and to lose yourself in the process. But what do you really want? Is it a supportive boss? The flexibility to pursue a hobby or pick your kids up from school? The potential to travel for work? Rank them by order of importance.

RANK

This is your story to tell.

What? So What? Now What? This model of reflection asks you to name the facts and feelings around a situation, to question the knowledge you had at the time and what else could help you make sense of it, and to create an action plan based on the two prior questions.[1] Apply these questions to your mindset.

WHAT IS YOUR CURRENT SITUATION?	HOW DID YOU GET HERE AND WHAT CAN YOU LEARN FROM IT?	WHAT CAN YOU DO ABOUT IT NOW?

Set up an informational interview at a company you have always been interested in. Meeting with someone who works in a field or position you're curious about is a smart way to gather information about what it's truly like to do that for a living and what it takes to land that type of position. Below, capture the questions you have for them and their responses. Once you've talked, are you still interested in that type of job?

YOUR QUESTIONS	THEIR RESPONSES

Your takeaway:

What will you miss about your last role? Even if you left or are planning to leave voluntarily, you may feel grief around the loss of routine, your favorite coworker, or this part of your identity.[2] It's important to honor those very real emotions. Use this space to reflect on them.

Revisit a time when the outcome was uncertain. Maybe it had to do with an idea you were pitching, a presentation you were giving, or a project that was reliant on other people's contributions to come together. What strategies did you use to get through that time?

How do you approach your work? Instead of hastily updating your resume or LinkedIn profile, first think about the words you use to describe your professional experience when talking about it. Jot them down, along with some of your latest big wins. It will be helpful to come back to them while working your way through Chapter 5.

DESCRIBE YOUR WORK

LATEST BIG WINS

Make a list of . . . emotions you're experiencing about your job search. You're no doubt working through a lot of feelings: excitement, uncertainty, frustration, anxiety, restlessness . . . exploring these in writing can help you process them, and better understand what you're going through.[3]

- ....
- ....
- ....
- ....
- ....
- ....
- ....
- ....
- ....

Where are these emotions coming from?

....

....

....

....

....

....

....

....

....

Reach out to someone who . . . you worked with at your last job. And then your last last job. And so on. Experts say it is these "weak ties" that are likely to land you your next job.[4] They can also offer perspective on your trajectory. Ask them where their career path has taken them. It will encourage you to you keep an open mind about where you're going.

2

GOAL SETTING

Work toward something tangible.

The only opportunities you have a shot at are the ones you go after. You've been focused on the number-one goal of getting a new job, but setting micro goals will be key to reaching it. The next set of prompts will encourage you to revisit past ambitions to inspire new ones.

Review your past reviews. What professional targets have you set for yourself in the past? Which did you meet, and which could you keep working toward now? Maybe you want to concentrate on your communication skills, or take an online course in a new certification.

PAST GOALS MET	GOALS TO KEEP WORKING TOWARD

What's an objective you'd like to set for the ever-elusive work–life balance? Is there anything you haven't been able to make the time for in life because of your work responsibilities? How might you remedy that in your next role?

Create a schedule for your job search and follow it. Routine produces results![1] It will also keep you from overthinking or spending all day hitting refresh. In addition to checking emails and job boards, build in time for exercise, being outdoors, working toward personal goals (see page 21), and anything else you want to make sure to enjoy outside of traditional working hours.

DAILY

5 AM ....

6 AM ....

7 AM ....

8 AM ....

9 AM ....

10 AM ....

11 AM ....

12 PM ....

1 PM ....

2 PM ....

3 PM ....

4 PM ....

5 PM ....

6 PM ....

7 PM ....

8 PM ....

WEEKLY

MONDAY

TUESDAY

WEDNESDAY

THURSDAY

FRIDAY

SATURDAY

SUNDAY

What are three goals you can set right now, completely separate from your job search? Write a book, develop an exercise regimen, plan a trip: These are for you, not to please or impress anyone else. Next, list the first steps you can take to reach them: Start an outline, do a five-minute bodyweight workout, follow a local hashtag for the place you'd like to visit.

Goal:

First step:

Goal:

First step:

Goal:

First step:

Now set three goals for your job search. Do you want to research new industries? Make new contacts? Start a newsletter? Outline your first steps for getting there.

Goal:

First step:

Goal:

First step:

Goal:

First step:

Identify a skill you want to learn or continue refining in your new job. Put aside quantifying your achievements with metrics for a moment. What abilities did you grow in your most recent job? What do you hope to learn next?

Reach out to someone who . . . can be an accountability partner. How do they like to track their progress?

What's something you can start and finish today? Cleaning out a drawer (or an entire closet, depending on your level of clutter), trying out a recipe, completing a crossword puzzle. Relish the sense of accomplishment.

What small wins have you experienced lately?

Celebrate all your milestones! What career and life achievements are you most proud of? What goals did you set along the way to get you there? What small wins have you experienced lately?

PAST ACHIEVEMENTS	HOW YOU GOT THERE	NEW SMALL WINS

3

EXPLORATION

Embrace the liminal space.

The unknown makes people uncomfortable.[1] But how you interpret this transitional period in your life, this liminal space, is an active choice. Think of how much you have to learn about yourself, the things you haven't had the time to try thus far. In this chapter, you will leave your schedule behind willingly and turn uncertainty into anticipation.

What's something you have always wanted to do during normal working hours? Take advantage of your free time while it lasts. Visit a museum, see a movie in the afternoon, set aside an hour to catch up with a friend. These adventures and experiences will fill your cup and may even spark some ideas about what you'd like to go back "on the clock" for.

Turn uncertainty

Build up your skillset while giving back. Volunteering not only looks great on a resume, it's also an opportunity to keep busy, help out, experience different work environments and working styles, and meet people. What are some places or causes you could contribute to?

into anticipation.

What are you afraid of? Hot sauce, roller coasters, making small talk: Choose your challenge and go for it. Making it through an unpleasant experience is a good reminder that you will make it through this one, and you're likely to come out of it with a good story. What happened when you took on something you feared?

Make a list of . . . hobbies you've always wanted to try or habits you'd like to adopt. Then get going on them. Meditating five minutes a day, baking bread, juggling, joining a pickup game?

Reach out to someone who . . . has had a career path that excites you. What steps did they take and what challenges did they face along the way? Ask them to include the ones that aren't on their resume.

Take a walk outside. Even just five minutes of walking in nature can boost your mood.[2] Changing your surroundings can change your perspective, and a walk can provide space to work through your thoughts. What came up for you?

Changing your surroundings can change your perspective.

Predict your future. Tap into your intuition. What do you think you will be doing four weeks from now? Four months from now? Be honest with yourself. The answer may surprise you.

FOUR WEEKS FROM NOW . . .

FOUR MONTHS FROM NOW . . .

Get out of your lane. Brainstorm industries and departments adjacent to your previous roles. Media → PR → Communications → Speechwriting. Sales → Strategy → Customer Service → Consulting. If you get stuck, AI tools can guide you in expanding your list. Where might a few degrees of separation take you?

.... → ....

→ .... → ....

.... → ....

→ .... → ....

.... → ....

→ .... → ....

.... → ....

→ .... → ....

Take a family member's work history. Who knows what common threads of interests, career paths, or roads less traveled their answers may uncover? Start with these questions and repeat as desired with other family members.

Name:

Career path:

What they liked:

What they didn't like:

Pivots during the course of their career:

Big moments:

Hardships or regrets:

Advice they would have given their younger self:

4

DREAM JOB

You will find the perfect job for you.

Work is an important part of our lives. For most of us, it fills many hours of our day, provides purpose, and helps us feel like productive members of society. Exploring what you'd really like to do, if there were no limits, allows you to envision what could be. Get ready to unlock prospects you've never even imagined . . . until now.

Write your dream job description. Some questions to consider: What responsibilities do you want to have? What type of interaction do you want to have with your coworkers? What areas do you want to grow in? How do you want to be compensated for your work?

Dress for the job you want. What does your go-to interview outfit say about you? Now think about how you would like to appear in your next position. Is there anything you can change up so that your look better conveys the image you want to present?

Go-to interview outfit

The new look you're going for

How do you feel in your new look?

Make a list of . . . perks that would make you perk up. Tuition reimbursement, ability to work abroad, wellness stipend, pawternity leave? What benefits would you put to good use? Now rank them in order of importance.

RANK

What did you want to be when you grew up? Use this space to examine what drew you to that ideal job. Uncovering the values that appealed to you as a child may help you envision what comes next in your adult life.

What does your ideal workday look like? Are you part of the morning dash to the office, coffee in hand? Or curled up on your couch ready to open your laptop? Spending the day using your hands? Crushing it in meetings? Is your afternoon free for brainstorming or does it end with a client dinner or event?

MORNING

LUNCH

AFTERNOON

EVENING

What are you looking for in a manager? Someone who has your back? Someone who mostly lets you do your own thing? Someone who emphasizes team building?

- ....
- ....
- ....
- ....
- ....
- ....
- ....
- ....
- ....
- ....
- ....
- ....

Uncovering the values that appealed to you as a child may help you envision what comes next in your adult life.

Reach out to someone who . . . has your dream job. What have you always wanted to know about that role? When you're ready, send them a brief note sharing your interest in their work. If you get the chance, ask them to share their favorite and least favorite parts of what they do for a living.

What you want to know about the job:

Their favorite and least favorite parts of the job:

What would you do with your time if you didn't have to earn money? Travel the world, go back to school, sleep in? How could your next job support these desires? A position that takes you to new places, offers a chance to audit classes, provides flexible working hours?

WHAT'S YOUR NEXT MOVE?

Review and reflect on your answers to the prompts in Part 1. How do they make you feel? What keywords keep coming up?

INTROSPECTION

GOAL SETTING

EXPLORATION

DREAM JOB

Is there anything you addressed here that you want to keep working on? What have you discovered that you want and need from your next role?

WHAT YOU NEED TO MAKE YOUR NEXT BIG CAREER MOVE

5

RESUME BUILDING

You are in control of your career and future.

Summarizing your work experience into bullet-pointed items and keywords that will catch the eye of a screener (human or computer) can be draining. You are so much more than a page—"or two, tops!" say most recruiters—of brief descriptions. But the resume is your chance to make a first impression, and those brief descriptions can have an impact. The prompts in this chapter will bring to light what makes you stand out.

Scan your resume for talking points. Which of those single lines about your responsibilities and accomplishments can serve as a launching point for a story that conveys who you are beyond your resume? Use this space to brainstorm a few ideas for your cover letter and interviews.

Ask for feedback. Have a colleague compare your resume to a job listing you're interested in and ask them what they'd do differently. You can also use AI tools to do this. (If companies are using AI to filter your resume, why not get some feedback from the filter itself? Just be careful not to over-genericize.) How might you change your approach based on what you have learned?

Assume you are sending your resume to someone who receives too many emails. Your cover letter is your chance to stand out, human to human. Limit yourself to three short paragraphs and leave the first sentence open for a personalized attention-grabbing line to show you've done your research about the position, company, and if possible, hiring manager. Brainstorm some opening lines here.

What past jobs and skills are you overlooking? Remember that summer spent slinging Cokes at baseball games? Customer service! Or that time you coordinated a family reunion? Problem solving! Regardless of where you learned them, all of your talents deserve a chance to shine as part of your application.

PAST JOB	HIDDEN TALENT

What points don't serve your objective? The job market is constantly evolving, and so are you. Experiences that felt important to share at a different stage of your career may now be stealing attention from more recent or relevant achievements. What outdated or irrelevant points can you edit out?

- ....
- ....
- ....
- ....
- ....
- ....
- ....
- ....

Describe your soft skills. Doing this is as important as listing your accomplishments. How might you highlight your communication, teamwork, and time management skills?

....

....

....

....

....

....

....

....

Make a list of . . . your transferrable skills. What are you really, really good at? What have your coworkers and managers complimented you on? Answering these questions will kickstart what is destined to become a very long list of talents, many of which will be useful to you regardless of the title of your next job.

- ....
- ....
- ....
- ....
- ....
- ....
- ....
- ....
- ....
- ....

What are you really, really good at?

Reach out to someone who . . . knows you personally and is familiar with the work that you do. Ask them to look over your resume. What five professions do they think you are qualified for, and why?

What was your favorite thing about the best job you ever had? The autonomy of a babysitting gig? Regular after-work gatherings with coworkers? Opportunities for bonuses? What positions might provide some of those opportunities, and what requirements and expertise are they looking for? Brainstorm how you can frame your resume to better suit those demands.

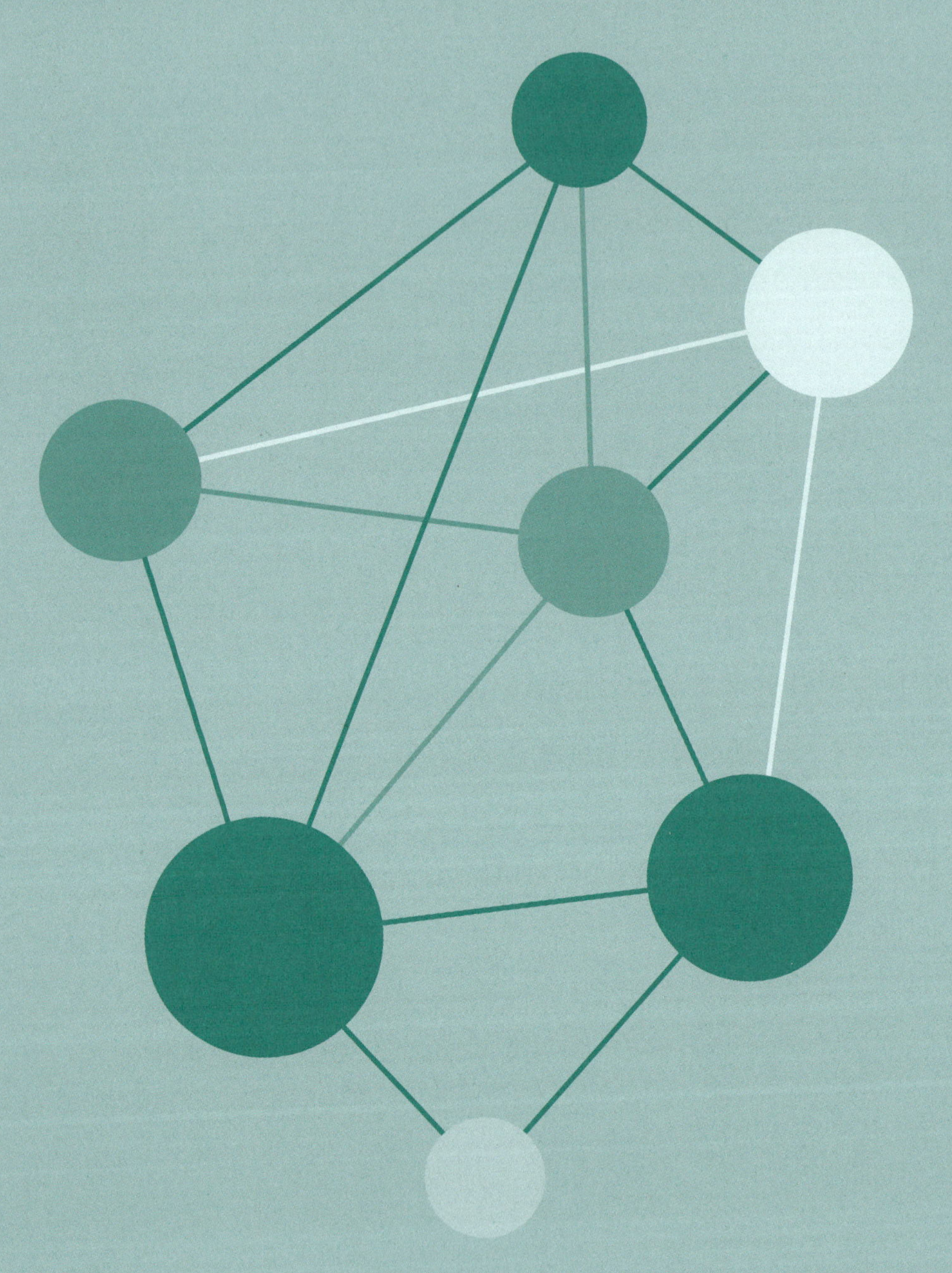

6

CONNECTION

You are not alone.

A job search doesn't have to feel like it's just you and your computer, taking on the world. There's no better time to reconnect with acquaintances, take stock of your everyday interactions, and meet new people. The best part? When you open up to others and share your experience, the possibilities are limitless.

Make a list of . . . people you know who recently found a job. It's a good reminder that you, too, will one day be on the other side of the search. Plus, learning about their career paths may inspire new thoughts about yours.

- ....
- ....
- ....
- ....
- ....
- ....
- ....
- ....
- ....
- ....
- ....

How can you get curious about someone else's experience today?

Who can you connect with online to expand your network? Think less about "five degrees of separation-ing" your way to your dream company and more about building on loose connections you may not have made the most of. Some to try:

Someone I enjoyed working with:

Someone from a completely different industry:

Someone I met in the past year but haven't kept up with:

Someone at a different stage of their career:

Curate your virtual space. Considering how easy it is to connect with people online, there's no reason not to set up lots of video chats—catch-ups, informational interviews, coworking on resumes. Make a to-do list for creating your ideal professional background, one that sells the image you want to present as a future employee. What might add dimension to the conversations you're having?

Attend an event hosted by a professional organization related to your industry. Spending time around people passionate about the same interests as you can be invigorating. What did you learn?

Practice being present in your conversations. Asking inquiring questions, noticing and acknowledging what makes someone special are ways to recognize others. In *How to Know a Person*, David Brooks says, "Human beings need recognition as much as they need food and water."[1] How can you get curious about someone else's experience today?

Post what you're up to. This isn't an #opentowork post, it's a life-beyond-work post. Maybe it's about one of those adventures you've been having, or goals you've been working toward, since reading Part 1. Maybe it's about something you read. The aim here is to share about yourself and engage with your professional community. Use a hashtag to reach more people, and try ending your post with a question to garner more responses. Write down what you learned.

Reach out to someone who . . . reacted to your post—ideally someone who you haven't spoken to in some time. What have they been doing lately?

Stick a name tag to your shirt. That's right, it's time to find a networking event. Aim for something tangential to the field you're interested in, or something related to a personal passion. Your goal: Speak to three people, record their information here, and then follow up with them via email or social media.

Name .... **Job** ....

Contact Information ....

Notes ....

....

....

....

Name .... **Job** ....

Contact Information ....

Notes ....

....

....

....

Name .... **Job** ....

Contact Information ....

Notes ....

....

....

....

Open yourself to spontaneous interaction. Consider a time when you tend to go insular—perhaps while on a walk, waiting in line, or on public transportation. This time, approach that situation as a chance to seek out a conversation with someone you encounter. You're likely to have a better time, and may even learn something.[2] Who did you meet? What did you discover?

7

INTERVIEW SKILLS

Keep your head in the game.

There are three components to a successful interview: belief in yourself, preparation, and flexibility. You need to be on top of your game, familiar with the company and role you're applying to, concise in your responses, and able to pivot on the fly. This goes way beyond reviewing the job description the night before. Using these prompts as practice, you will be more than ready when you get there.

Tell me about yourself in 60 seconds. Communicating clearly and concisely is important on and off the job. Write down your talking points, set a timer, and keep trying till you get it down, crossing out sections and rewriting to hone your answer.

Brainstorm small-talk subjects. Display your leadership by helping to eliminate awkward pre-interview silence. New skills, shared connections, and interesting news tidbits (industry or general interest) are all game. Jot down five potential conversation starters here.

Look into a company you're interested in. Or research general industry trends. Press releases, news searches, and LinkedIn profiles are all good places to start. What's something you learned?

Read something to expand your mindset. Choose something professional (a trade website or newsletter) and something else more personal (like a hashtag that will keep you up-to-date with news of the latest gardening trends/pickleball matches/you name it). What's something you picked up that you could share in an interview?

Share a real weakness and how you're working on it. We all know the interview question about our weaknesses, and many of us have been led to believe that providing a strength disguised as a weakness is the answer. However, as Brene Brown says in *The Power of Vulnerability*, innovation and adaptability start with lowering your defenses.[1] Showing up authentically at the interview is a great starting point.

Reach out to someone who . . . has recently been interviewing. What have they noticed about the hiring process lately, and what questions do they like to ask of a future employer?

Make a list of . . . points on what you really want to know about a future employer. Is the environment collaborative or competitive? Will your manager be supportive of your growth? Remember, this isn't only about your impressing them. Interviewing is also about determining whether this is a good fit for you.

- ....
- ....
- ....
- ....
- ....
- ....
- ....
- ....
- ....
- ....

Interviewing is also about determining whether this is a good fit for you.

What's the one question you're most afraid of being asked? Take some time to think about why, then move on to how you could answer it, and write your response here.

The question that scares you:

What it brings up:

How you can answer it:

WHAT'S YOUR NEXT MOVE?

Review and reflect on your answers to the prompts in Part 2. How do they make you feel? What keywords keep coming up?

RESUME BUILDING

CONNECTION

INTERVIEW SKILLS

Is there anything you addressed here that you want to keep working on? How are you actively building the skills to help land your next role?

HOW YOU STAY FOCUSED ON YOUR NEXT BIG CAREER MOVE

8

MOTIVATION

Work through the wait.

The job market can be tough, and the job search process can feel repetitive and exhausting. Moving forward is the only option. That moment you feel like you've hit a wall is exactly the time when you have to dig deep to find your drive. In this chapter, you'll build up your mental strength and the endurance to keep going, even on those days when it feels like you've already done all you could possibly do.

Make a list of . . . strategies that have helped you stay positive. Do you have more energy for tackling cover letters in the morning? How do you keep your mind occupied while waiting for responses? Do you have a go-to follow-up email subject line that yields quick results?

What role has your job played in your identity and purpose? Our identities are increasingly defined by our work.[1] How has what you do for work influenced your self-worth? Is your job the first thing you bring up in conversation, or the last? Would you like that to change? How might you adjust your job search to address that?

Reach out to someone who . . . has already accomplished something professionally that you one day hope to do. What do they want to do next?

Recharge. It takes a lot to put yourself out there. It's time to do something that makes you feel good. Cook your favorite meal, take a long walk, meet up with a friend. How do you feel after taking some time for yourself? How can you build something like this into your schedule every few days?

That moment you feel like you've hit a wall is exactly the time when you have to dig deep to find your drive.

What gets you excited about your work? The thrill of the sale? Helping people? Focusing on the parts of work that light you up will save you from wasting energy on listings that won't be satisfying.

Who might you ask to be a mentor? Think of a few people you admire who you can check in with semi-regularly. A professional contact who has more experience can provide perspective on where you are and where you're headed.

Get moving. Physical movement has been linked to motivation.[2] The next time you feel like picking up your phone for a break, instead take a few minutes to stretch or wake yourself up with some jumping jacks. Haven't exercised in a while? Chair yoga is a simple habit-forming practice that you can do just about anywhere. After trying it for a few days, how do you feel?

Take a few minutes to stretch.

What do you want the first day at your new job to look like? Envision it—what impression do you want to make on your coworkers? What would you like to learn? How can you keep this front of mind during your job search?

Write a note to your future self who has been at your new job for one year. What do you hope to be celebrating?

9

CONFIDENCE

There's only one you.

Knocking on doors (literally or figuratively) is hard work that can make you doubt your abilities and your worthiness. This chapter is the equivalent of listening to your favorite high-energy song before a big meeting. The prompts here will encourage you, reassure you, and give you the support and conviction to keep putting yourself out there.

Who are your hype people? These are the people who know you best and are always happy to remind you just how great you are. Check in with them regularly—their encouragement will go a long way toward keeping your spirits up.

- ....
- ....
- ....
- ....
- ....
- ....
- ....
- ....

Make a list of . . . pump-up songs. Turn to these whenever you need a mood boost, like when you're getting ready for all of your upcoming interviews.

- ....
- ....
- ....
- ....
- ....
- ....
- ....
- ....
- ....

Learn something new. Acquiring a skill builds confidence and keeps you adaptable.[1] What might you take a crack at?

- ....
- ....
- ....
- ....
- ....
- ....
- ....
- ....
- ....
- ....
- ....
- ....
- ....
- ....
- ....
- ....
- ....
- ....
- ....
- ....
- ....
- ....

Reach out to someone who . . . you admire for the way they carry themselves—the person who is on top of everything at work, someone who always presents a positive, can-do attitude. Ask them about a time they had to build themselves up.

When was the last time your confidence took a hit? How can you reframe that experience? Psychologist Dr. Jenny Wang says the most successful people are able to focus on how failure has helped them.[2] But don't be too hard on yourself if it doesn't come instantly. This is a learned skill.

Take an audit of your body language. What message is it sending yourself and others? In her book *Presence*, social psychologist Amy Cuddy says, "How you carry yourself—your facial expressions, your postures, your breathing—all clearly affect the way you think, feel, and behave."[3] Smiling, rolling back your shoulders, and straightening your spine are easy ways to communicate the assurance you want to feel and project.

Know your worth. Research salary ranges for the jobs you're interested in. Ask others in your field how much they make (people who have recently left a company may be more willing to share this), what their schedule was like, and what benefits made a difference in their lives. Pump yourself up to name your number (subject to reviewing the whole package) when the time comes.

SALARY

SCHEDULE

BENEFITS

PAID TIME OFF

Say yes to the next invitation extended to you. Whether it's to a charity event, a dinner, or more syrup on your pancakes, throw yourself in fully with openness to exploring the potential. How did it go?

What's your superpower? Have you been a natural-born salesperson since your first lemonade stand? Are you a tinkerer who needs to know the ins and outs of everything you work on? Reflect on your incredible ability here.

Throw yourself in with full confidence and openness to exploring the potential.

10

GRATITUDE

This is the best thing that will ever happen to you. Really.

There are so many things to be grateful for. People, experiences, even just having this time to summon all the circumstances that brought you here, the memories they bring up, and the potential to lay the path for what comes next with gratitude for what came before. Thank goodness.

Who is the first person who took a chance on you at work? This could be someone who nurtured your potential, the first person who ever hired you, or someone who taught you a skill. Use this space to write down what that meant to you—and then be sure to follow up and let them know.

Name at least three things you can express gratitude for today.

Adopting this habit has been proven to enhance health and happiness.[1] Record if you have noticed any changes in your thinking. Repeat for at least the next two days.

DAY 1

1. ....

2. ....

3. ....

....

....

DAY 2

1. ....

2. ....

3. ....

....

....

DAY 3

1. ....

2. ....

3. ....

....

....

Look for the upside of your setbacks. This valuable skill is a cornerstone of a growth mindset: the belief, popularized by psychologist Carol Dweck, that talent can be developed through hard work, good strategies, and feedback from others.[2] Write about one of your hard times. What value did it ultimately have for you?

It's never too late to acknowledge someone.

Send a handwritten thank you note. Putting pen to paper helps you to slow down and really think about what you want to say, and a handwritten note makes an impression on the recipient.[3] It's never too late to acknowledge someone. Draft your message here, and then transfer it to a proper note—envelope, stamp, and all.

Offer your help to someone else. Give the gift of free time to someone who's feeling overwhelmed, or the gift of your expertise to a local organization. Clean out a closet at home and donate anything you haven't used in a year. Work giving back into your regular routine. Reflect on the experience below.

What's something you're looking forward to when you start your new role? Gratitude isn't only about reflecting on the past and appreciating the present. It also encompasses having a hopeful view of the future.

Make a list of . . . people who have been an important part of your career journey. What do you want to thank them for?

PEOPLE TO THANK	WHAT TO THANK THEM FOR

Reach out to someone who . . . you included in your list on the previous page. What have they been grateful for over the course of their career?

Put a reminder in your pocket. Spend some time searching for quotes about gratitude. Record the ones that resonate here. Now choose your favorite in this moment, make a copy, and put it somewhere you will be reminded of it often. Notice how seeing it impacts your outlook and your actions.

11

ADAPTABILITY

Your ability to adjust will lead to more opportunities.

We're living in a time of constant change, and employers are looking for candidates who can adapt.[1] Staying agile won't just benefit your future employer; it's a step toward your own growth and expansion.[2] The following prompts will stretch your flexibility muscle.

Switch something up. Make a slight shift to your morning routine, head to a different job site than your usual go-to, take a walk around the block at a time when you're normally inside. What do you notice? How did it feel? What other practices or assumptions could use some shaking up?

Reach out to someone who . . . has recently switched departments or, better yet, industries. What prompted the change and what has helped them with the adjustment?

Make a list of . . . moments when you have adjusted to unexpected change. You've likely navigated this more times than you realize.

- ....
- ....
- ....
- ....
- ....
- ....
- ....
- ....

What strategies helped you get through those moments, and which can you draw on again?

Apply for a role you're interested in but meet less than half the qualifications for. Adapting your resume and cover letter for it will uncover skills you may want to focus on learning next. Record those here, along with any other roles and terms you want to add to your search keywords.

Visit somewhere new today. This could be the next city over or somewhere farther. Traveling somewhere you have never been (even virtually through Google Streetview) is the quickest way to expand your world and escape your comfort zone. Where did you go and what did you learn?

Traveling somewhere you have way to expand your world and

Acknowledge that adapting can be stressful. How do you tend to cope with the stress that comes with change? Are there any additional approaches you'd like to try? How can you put them into practice?

never been is the quickest

escape your comfort zone.

Think of a time when you have practiced being open-minded. Maybe you sat in on an open meeting at work to observe a different way of doing things. Maybe you went to an event where you didn't know anyone. How could the same attitude benefit your job search?

How have your thoughts about work evolved over the course of working through this journal? If your values have shifted, or haven't been reflected in your roles up to this point, how might you adjust your job search to better suit you?

WHAT'S YOUR NEXT MOVE?

Review and reflect on your answers to the prompts in Part 3. How do they make you feel? What keywords keep coming up?

MOTIVATION

CONFIDENCE

GRATITUDE

ADAPTABILITY

Is there anything you addressed here that you want to keep working on? What will keep you moving toward your goals?

YOUR NEXT BIG CAREER MOVE IS UP TO YOU

I hope that as you complete this journal you feel more clarity about what you want to do next, and in more control of your job and career and how you approach them. When I started writing this journal, I was a little bit lost. I was trying to make sense of who I was apart from my job, to figure out what options I had, and I felt a strong pull to help others in the same situation.

One year out from the layoff that started it all, beyond landing a fantastic new job, I've connected and reconnected with a great number of people, had many meaningful interviews, received multiple offers, and gained a ton of work and life experience. It's like I wrote in Chapter 8: Moving forward is the only option.

The rest is up to you. No job is perfect, no career trajectory is a straight line, but now that you have completed ninety-nine prompts about yourself, your work experience, your goals, and your dreams, you're in the best possible position to decide what comes next.

If this journal helped you, please drop me a line at yournextbigcareermove@gmail.com

NOTES

Introduction

1. Jennifer Parris, "How Long Should a Job Search Take?," *FlexJobs*, accessed July 18, 2025, flexjobs.com/blog/post/how-long-should-a-job-search-take.
2. "Breaking the cycle of grief after a layoff," Aerotek, November 13, 2018, aerotek.com/en/insights/breaking-the-cycle-of-grief-after-a-layoff.

1. Introspection

1. "What? So what? Now what?," Reflectors' Toolkit: Reflecting on experience, the University of Edinburgh, October 15, 2024, reflection.ed.ac.uk/reflectors-toolkit/reflecting-on-experience/what-so-what-now-what.
2. Erica Brown, "Job Loss Is a Kind of Grief," *The Atlantic*, March 28, 2025, theatlantic.com/ideas/archive/2025/03/job-loss-shiva/682208.
3. Kim Mills, host, *Speaking of Psychology*, episode 277, "Expressive writing can help your mental health, with James Pennebaker, PhD," American Psychological Association, March 13, 2024, 43 min., apa.org/news/podcasts/speaking-of-psychology/expressive-writing.
4. Karen Wickre, *Taking the Work Out of Networking: Your Guide to Making and Keeping Great Connections* (Touchstone, 2018), 47–55.

2. Goal Setting

1. Steve Alexander Jr., "The Importance of Routines in Pursuit of Your Goals," *Psychology Today*, November 7, 2021, psychologytoday.com/us/blog/opening-the-door/202111/the-importance-routines-in-pursuit-your-goals.

3. Exploration

1. D. W. Grupe and J. B. Nitschke, "Uncertainty and anticipation in anxiety: an integrated neurobiological and psychological perspective," *Nature Reviews Neuroscience* 14 (2013): 488–501, doi:10.1038/nrn3524.
2. "Nature Makes You . . . ," National Park Service, accessed July 13, 2025, nps.gov/articles/naturesbenefits.htm.

6. Connection

1. David Brooks, *How to Know a Person: The Art of Seeing Others Deeply and Being Deeply Seen* (Random House, 2023), 9.
2. J. Schroeder, D. Lyons, and N. Epley, "Hello, stranger? Pleasant conversations are preceded by concerns about starting one," *Journey of Experimental Psychology: General* 151, no. 5 (2022): 1141–53.

7. Interview Skills

1. Brene Brown, *The Power of Vulnerability: Teachings on Authenticity, Connection, and Courage* (Sounds True, 2012).

8. Motivation

1. Derek Thompson, "Workism Is Making Americans Miserable," *The Atlantic*, February 24, 2019, theatlantic.com/ideas/archive/2019/02/religion-workism-making-americans-miserable/583441.
2. David Orenstein, "Study finds hub linking movement and motivation in the brain," *MIT News*, September 19, 2019, news.mit.edu/2019/study-finds-hub-linking-movement-and-motivation-brain-0919.

9. Confidence

1. "The mind-body benefits of learning a new skill," Piedmont Healthcare, accessed March 25, 2025, piedmont.org/living-real-change/the-mind-body-benefits-of-learning-a-new-skill.
2. Dr. Jenny Wang, "A psychologist says the most successful people 'reframe failure' by doing 4 things," *CNBC Make It*, May 18, 2022, cnbc.com/2022/05/18/a-psychologist-says-the-most-successful-people-reframe-failure-by-doing-4-things.html.
3. Amy Cuddy, *Presence: Bringing Your Boldest Self to Your Biggest Challenges* (Little, Brown Spark, 2018), 192.

10. Gratitude

1. Maureen Salamon, "Gratitude enhances health, brings happiness—and may even lengthen lives," *Harvard Health Publishing*, September 11, 2024, health.harvard.edu/blog/gratitude-enhances-health-brings-happiness-and-may-even-lengthen-lives-202409113071.
2. Carol Dweck, "What Having a Growth Mindset Actually Means," *Harvard Business Review*, January 13, 2016, hbr.org/2016/01/what-having-a-growth-mindset-actually-means.
3. Jonathan Lambert, "Why writing by hand beats typing for thinking and learning," *Shots: Health News from NPR*, May 11, 2024, npr.org/sections/health-shots/2024/05/11/1250529661/handwriting-cursive-typing-schools-learning-brain; Shivani Vora, "Do Thank-You Notes Still Matter?," *The New York Times*, updated December 21, 2022, nytimes.com/2022/11/15/style/why-thank-you-notes.html.

11. Adaptability

1. Alejandro Oses, "Most In Demand Skills for Employers as We Enter 2025," *Forbes*, October 30, 2024, forbes.com/councils/forbestechcouncil/2024/10/30/most-in-demand-skills-for-employers-as-we-enter-2025.
2. Dr. Taryn Marie Stejskal, *The 5 Practices of Highly Resilient People* (Hachette Go, 2023), xi.

ACKNOWLEDGMENTS

To Lia, who said "my mom's great at writing books," which inspired me to give it a shot.

To Rory, who has been by my side through it all, including layoffs, moments when I wanted to quit and rethink my entire career, and title and cover brainstorming.

To Mom and Dad, who said the next job will be better, and asked, "Why don't you work on that book idea to help other people in the same situation?"

To Leanne and Rach, who said they thought people would be relieved to find a book like this.

To my friends, family, and neighbor crew for their support, interest, and willingness to answer countless questions about their work experience.

To Lynn, who took me to breakfast on my last day of work and said, "This is the best thing that will ever happen to you."

To Sara, who saw the need for a resource like this, a way to expand the readership, and kept making it better with each pass.

To Matthew, Peter, and everyone else at The Experiment who helped to create this and get the word out, including Beth, Zach, Ally, and Besse.

To Karen, who taught Career and Life Choices at UMass—a class I still think about—and took the time to reconnect twenty years later and continue the conversation.

To those who read early drafts and offered feedback, advice, and words of support.

To the Maplewood Library for making so many research titles accessible. To the Brooklyn Public Library for giving me one of my first jobs.

To you, who made it this far. Thank you for reading and journaling.

ABOUT THE AUTHOR

CARA BEDICK is an editor who has published hundreds of self-help, business, lifestyle, and motivational books, including several international bestsellers. A trendspotter and entrepreneur by nature, she has been featured in *The New York Times*, *Publishers Weekly*, *The Information*, *Restaurant Business*, *The San Diego Union Tribune*, and more. She was a featured speaker at Skillshare's 2024 "Dream Job Week" and speaks regularly at conferences, including American Society of Journalists and Authors, *Writer's Digest*, and the Pacific Northwest Writers Association. *Your Next Big Career Move* is her first book.

carabedick.com | @carabedick